Marvels in the Muck

Life in the Salt Marshes

Doug Wechsler

BOYDS MILLS PRESS

HONESDALE, PENNSYLVANIA

For Mike Lederberg, a great friend, who accompanied me
on my earliest forays into salt marshes many years ago

ACKNOWLEDGMENTS

I am indebted to Dr. Richard J. Horwitz of the Academy of Natural
Sciences of Philadelphia for reviewing the science in the book. Thanks
to Betty Tatham for helpful comments on the manuscript. My editor,
Andy Boyles, greatly improved the section on tides. Scott and Joseph
Yeager kindly allowed me to photograph both of them in the marsh.
My greatest debt is to my wife, Debbie, who endured occasional clouds
of biting midges, marauding greenheads, and a lot of waiting and who
helped me paddle our canoe to many of the remote parts of the salt
marshes that we both love.

—D.W.

Text and photographs copyright © 2008 by Doug Wechsler
All rights reserved

Boyds Mills Press, Inc.
815 Church Street
Honesdale, Pennsylvania 18431
Printed in China

Library of Congress Cataloging-in-Publication Data

Wechsler, Doug.
  Marvels in the muck : life in the salt marshes / Doug Wechsler. — 1st ed.
    p. cm.
  ISBN 978-1-59078-588-1 (hardcover : alk. paper)
  1. Salt marsh ecology—Juvenile literature. 2. Salt marshes—Juvenile
literature. I. Title.

  QH541.5.S24W43 2008
  578.769—dc22
                              2007052583

First edition
Designed by Tim Gillner
The text of this book is set in 12-point Palatino.

10 9 8 7 6 5 4 3 2 1

Contents

Snow geese land in the marsh to feed on cordgrass.

Introduction

A creek meanders through an icy winter salt marsh.

Northern Winter

IT SOUNDED LIKE A CROWD CHEERING at a baseball game. Far out in the wintry brown and black salt marsh, what looked like a cloud of snowflakes rose into the air. Actually, they were snow geese—a flock of thousands.

If it weren't for geese and other birds, the New Jersey salt marsh would seem almost dead in winter. Much of the other marsh life has either gone elsewhere or is hiding. Fiddler crabs winter in burrows beneath the mud. Mummichogs, small marsh-dwelling fish, move into salt marsh pools and hide in the mud during the coldest weather. Blue crabs move into deeper water and become inactive, burrowing into the mud or sand for the winter.

Have you ever been to a salt marsh? If you have visited a beach on the East Coast or Gulf Coast of the United States, you probably passed right through or over a salt marsh. Salt marshes grow in bays and along creeks and rivers that flow into salt water. Salt marshes are wetlands with grasses and low-growing plants that are flooded by the tides. Salt marshes grow in places that are protected from powerful waves. They do best where the water is brackish—that is, less salty than the ocean, but not fresh enough to drink.

Tides are the daily rising and falling of the level of the sea. In the salt marsh, the water rises during high tide, covering the grass. Then at low tide the water flows out, leaving the whole marsh above the water level. Bays, lagoons, and river mouths, where fresh water mixes with salt water, are places of abundant life called estuaries. A salt marsh is part of an estuary, and the growth of the marsh feeds the estuary.

The East Coast and Gulf Coast of the United States have some of the largest salt marshes in the world. On the Pacific Coast, there are fewer protected waters where salt marshes can grow. West Coast marshes are mostly small and scattered.

Small geese called brant spend the winter in salt marshes and on mud flats.

Birds Bring Winter Cheer

In winter, salt marshes feed huge flocks of snow geese, small white geese with black wing tips. These hardy birds breed in Arctic Canada and migrate south into salt marshes and other large marshes for winter. They feed on underground stems and roots of cordgrass. Often the flocks are made up of thousands of geese. There are so many snow geese in some places that they harm the marsh by eating it down to bare mud.

Another small goose, the brant, is common in many salt marshes in winter. This dark goose with a black head and neck, dark gray-brown back, and white rear end travels in smaller flocks. It eats sea lettuce (an alga) and cordgrass in the marsh and chows down on eelgrass from nearby bays. Like the snow goose, it migrates to the Arctic in summer.

Many ducks also spend winter in the marsh. If you take a boat down the salt marsh creeks, you are likely to see such species as black duck, mallard, and green-winged teal. Many other species feed in and around the marsh. Black ducks are the most common marsh breeders in the North. They are particularly fond of eating snails. On the Gulf Coast and in Florida, mottled ducks replace black ducks as the common salt marsh duck.

Predators and Prey

Where marshes teem with geese and ducks, chances are bald eagles will be nearby, thinking, "Lunch." Bald eagles like an easy meal, such as a duck or goose wounded by a hunter. They often steal fish from ospreys. An eagle will dive at an osprey until the smaller bird drops its fish. Bald eagles also eat dead fish. Eagles are quite capable of catching healthy ducks, geese, and fish as well. Bald eagles disappeared from most of the East Coast in the 1950s and 1960s, when the pesticide DDT was frequently sprayed to kill mosquitoes and caterpillars. Since DDT was banned in the 1970s, the number of eagles has grown. Now bald eagles soar over most large marshes.

This herring gull is not too pleased to have a peregrine falcon nearby.

Large numbers of shorebirds and small ducks, such as green-winged teal, will attract the fastest of all birds of prey, the peregrine falcon. Peregrine falcons often fly high above the marsh, hunting for birds. When they spot a flock of sandpipers, the falcons will dive, sometimes faster than 150 mph. When sandpipers spot a peregrine overhead, they will often fly close to one another in a tight ball. The sandpipers turn together in perfect synchrony. At one moment you see their dark backs and at the next, their white bellies. This makes it hard for the falcon to pick out a single victim. If one sandpiper is separated from the flock, it is more likely to become prey to the falcon.

While most sandpipers have flown farther south for the winter, one species of sandpiper still visits the mud flats in large numbers. Dunlin are now looking very dull in their winter plumage. They form flocks of hundreds, keeping a wary eye out for peregrine falcons. The dunlin will stay until it is time to migrate to the Arctic in spring.

In northern salt marshes, the dunlin is the only kind of sandpiper to brave the winter in large numbers.

A laughing gull in breeding colors yawns.

Chapter 1

Sandpipers such as this short-billed dowitcher spend much time foraging on mud flats in the marsh.

SPRING
Return of the Laughing Gulls

Ha-ha-ha-haaah-haaah. The laughing call of a gull overhead is the first sign of spring in this New Jersey salt marsh. Laughing gulls are migrating from shores and marshes farther south. With their black heads, gray backs, white breasts, and red bills and legs, these are the most handsome gulls of the salt marsh. More than any other gulls, laughing gulls need salt marshes to survive. Follow the laughing gulls, and you will learn a great deal about their marshy home.

Battered brown grasses are what the laughing gull sees below. Last year's growth of grasses is slowly breaking down. New green shoots will soon pop through. In the marsh, a flock of brant feed on algae. The water is cold. Early spring is a pleasant time to visit the salt marsh. Days are getting warmer, but not yet warm enough to bring out the hoards of hungry mosquitoes and biting flies.

Smooth cordgrass provides both shelter and building material for a clapper rail nest.

King of Grasses

The brown grass that the laughing gulls see is called cordgrass. Scientists call the grass *Spartina*. By midspring, new grass leaves will start to turn the marsh green. When the gulls settle down to breed, they will nest in the cordgrass. So will many other marsh birds. The gulls even use dead cordgrass to build their nest.

Of all the plants that grow in the mud of the salt marsh, one species of cordgrass, smooth cordgrass, stands out as king. In the deepest parts of the marsh, called the low marsh, this is often the only kind of plant you can find. Smooth cordgrass is usually between two and six feet high (sixty centimeters to two meters), though it can shoot up as tall as nine feet (almost three meters). In the high marsh, closer to shore, it grows tall along the creeks and shorter on flat places that are flooded for briefer periods of time. From southern Canada to northern Florida and along many parts of the Gulf Coast of the United States, this one kind of plant makes up most of the marsh.

A salt marsh creek, or gut, flows in late winter.

Why does this one plant take up so much space? Smooth cordgrass is better adapted than any other marsh plant to living in salt water. Its roots stop much of the salt from entering the plant. It also has special glands on its leaves that excrete, or get rid of, salt. If you look closely at the leaves, you can see the salt grains.

Cordgrass can grow well in marsh mud, which has little oxygen below the surface. Plants, like animals, need oxygen to live. Cordgrass has special ducts, or tubes, that act like snorkels to carry oxygen down into the roots. Some of that oxygen leaks out from the roots, changing iron in the mud into a form that is useful to the plant.

Marsh Mud

As the tide goes down, laughing gulls scan for food on the mud flats at the edge of the marsh and along its creeks. Mud flats are wide areas of mud in estuaries that are exposed at low tide. Gulls hunting on the flats are often rewarded with worms, crabs, or, with luck, a dead fish.

Mummichogs are often incredibly abundant in salt marshes.

Salt marsh mud flats are exposed at low tide.

A semipalmated plover pulls a large worm from the mud.

Mud in the marsh is exposed at low tide. Mud is murky, mucky, and yucky, and it stinks, sticks, and stains. But without it, there would be no marsh. Mud is a mixture of water, clay, fine bits of soil, and tiny pieces of rotted plants and animals. Mud holds the nutrients that plants need. Nutrients are chemicals that help things grow. Many tiny animals live in mud, munching the decomposing plants and animals along with the decomposers—bacteria and fungi.

Along the muddy-banked, meandering marsh creeks, a flock of dunlin—a species of sandpiper with a beautiful reddish back in spring—are feeding on worms and crustaceans. They probe for food, moving their heads up and down, driving their long bills into the mud like sewing machine needles punching into cloth. Their sensitive beak tips can feel, much as your fingertips do. Mud may be a dirty word to you, but to dunlin it is a restaurant.

Mud is home to many invertebrates, animals without backbones, such as clams, marine worms, and little shrimplike creatures called amphipods. Mud even protects the marsh by keeping out people who might trample or drive through it. Mud in the salt marsh can be dangerous. In some places, it is easy to sink to the top of your legs. People who become stuck in the muck can have a hard time getting out, so don't wander around the marsh alone!

Great egrets, snowy egrets, and laughing gulls gather to feed on mummichogs in a salt marsh creek.

Up and Down with the Tides

When the tide is low, laughing gulls fly to the small creeks in the salt marsh. Small killifish called mummichogs are easy to catch when the water is shallow. They swarm in the little creeks, where they are prey for herons, egrets, ibises, and gulls. The lives of mummichogs, gulls, and all of the other creatures of the marsh are ruled by the cycle of tides.

In fact, without the tides, the salt marsh would not exist. The flow of salt water in and out of the estuary creates the special conditions needed for a salt marsh to form. What drives the cycle of the tides? The gravity of the moon and the sun pulling on the earth causes the tides. (See "What Causes the Tides?" on page 46 to learn how this works.)

On the Atlantic Coast, tides rise and fall twice a day. Well, almost twice a day. A full cycle from high tide to low tide is about 12 hours and 25 minutes. That means it takes 24 hours and 50 minutes to complete two cycles. So to pursue killifish at low tide, gulls must hunt for them 50 minutes later each day. On the Gulf Coast, tides sometimes rise and fall only once over the same period of time.

What do the tides do for the marsh? From a gull's point of view, they bring in the groceries and take out the garbage. The tides carry water in and out of the marsh. With the water come delicious fish and nutrients that the animals and grasses need. As the water goes out, it sweeps away dead grasses that otherwise might smother the marsh.

At low tide, grasses and mud can get plenty of oxygen from the air and warmth from the sun. Birds can feed from the mud flats, shallow streams, and pools.

As the tide rises, fish swim in to feed in the marsh. Saltwater turtles called diamondback terrapins swim up salt marsh creeks to feed and bask in the sun. Extra salt that has dried on the grasses washes off. Mussels and other shellfish in the marsh can feed by filtering particles out of the water.

Food Chains: Who Eats Whom?

The sun has a small effect on the tides but a huge effect on life in the marsh. Plants use the energy of the sun to grow. There are no trees in the marsh, so the cordgrass and other marsh plants get full sun and all the water they need to grow quickly.

How does cordgrass feed the estuary? The story starts when a blade of cordgrass dies. It soon becomes food for fungi and bacteria. Fungi grow inside the blade as tiny strands. Sometimes you can see black dots on the leaves of the dead cordgrass, which are the reproductive parts of the fungi. Fungi break up the tough cellulose that holds the grass together. At the same time, bacteria are also feeding on the leaf, decomposing it.

The fungi, bacteria, and rotting leaf together make a nice meal for fiddler crabs, which use their claws to pick up bits

A Salt Marsh Food Chain

1. *Smooth cordgrass grows using energy from the sun and nutrients from the marsh.*

2. *Fungi decompose the grass.*

3. *Fiddler crabs eat detritus, which includes decomposing cordgrass.*

4. *Diamondback terrapins eat fiddler crabs.*

5. *Herring gulls eat small diamondback terrapins.*

of decomposing leaves and put them into their mouths. Male fiddler crabs have one huge claw and one small one. They use the big claw to wave and signal to females. They eat using only the small claw. Female fiddlers can use both claws separately and can eat twice as fast.

After crabs have eaten rotten cordgrass along with the fungi and bacteria, turtles swim into the marsh to eat the crabs. Diamondback terrapins are salad-plate-sized turtles that live only in salt marshes and mangroves—habitats of salt-loving trees that grow in estuaries of southern Florida and southern Texas. In fact, these terrapins are the only turtles normally found in salt marshes. When a small turtle is basking onshore, a herring gull may swoop down and carry it off for a meal.

At the top of this food chain is the herring gull, which eats the turtle that ate the crabs that ate the fungi and bacteria along with the cordgrass. If this large gull is healthy, it is big enough to escape or defend itself from just about any other predator in the salt marsh.

Chains to Webs

That is just one food chain. There are many, many others in the salt marsh. Usually these chains start with cordgrass or with algae that grow on the mud or at the base of the cordgrass. For example, the algae are munched on by grass shrimp, which are eaten by mummichogs, which are eaten by herring gulls. Now the two food chains are joined since both end with herring gulls on top. If you keep studying these chains, you will see a whole web of predators and prey. This is the food web. It all starts with the energy from the sun. That energy is passed from plant, to plant eater, to predator, and finally to decomposer.

All of the energy captured by cordgrass does not stay in the marsh. Much of it moves out into the rest of the estuary. Many types of fish use the marsh as a nursery. Some of these fish are born in the marsh, but surprisingly, many find their way to marshes after being born at sea. At this stage of their

Follow the arrows from the food or prey to the animal that eats it. Each pathway from the bottom to the top is a food chain. All of the connections together make up the food web. When animals at the top of the web die, decomposers will turn them into detritus and start the cycle over.

lives, they look very different from their parents and are called larvae. When the baby fish get older, they move out of the marsh into the estuary or the ocean beyond. Blue crabs spend much of their time in the marsh but move out to breed in deeper water. And let's not forget the crab, fish, worm, and bird poop. Much of that waste flows out of the marsh with the tide. Nutrients from poop are used by algae growing in the bay, which, in turn, feed another food chain there.

Life in the whole estuary depends on the marsh. We rely on food from the estuary that gets its food directly or indirectly

A diamondback terrapin swims up a marsh creek as the tide rises.

from the marsh. The energy we get from eating flounder, crab, oysters, clams, shrimp, and many other types of seafood comes partly from the sun hitting that blade of cordgrass.

Marsh Madness

As days get longer and warmer in midspring, the marsh comes to life. Suddenly the air is full of birdsong. Added to the laughter of the gulls is the chuckling *kek-kek-kek-kek-kek* of the clapper rail, the *witchity-witchity-witchity* of the common yellowthroat, and the *con-ker-reee* of the red-winged blackbird.

Diamondback terrapins are basking in the sun on the banks of creeks. They need the spring sun's warmth to help them digest food. Not too long ago, people ate terrapins in large numbers. Hunting terrapins is not nearly as common now, but they still face quite a few enemies when they come onto land—raccoons, dogs, foxes, and, worst of all, automobiles. Cars squash thousands of female terrapins that come onto land to lay their eggs in late spring.

Birds suddenly seem to be everywhere. Migrants are pouring in from as far away as the southern tip of South America. Many birds will stay and breed in the marsh. Others will feed for a while and move on. Some travel another two thousand miles to raise their young in the Arctic.

A great egret stalks fish.

22

Birds are the most visible animals in the salt marsh. Herons and egrets stand tall above the shorter marsh grasses and are the easiest birds to spot. Birds come to feed on the abundant fish and invertebrates. Only a few birds live in the salt marsh all year, and some of these are never found outside the salt marsh.

Snowy egrets (left) are often quite lively while foraging.

Reddish egrets (right) are the dancers of the southern salt marsh.

Stalkers and Dancers

A great egret, bright white and nearly three feet (about one meter) tall, can be spotted nearly a mile (about one and a half kilometers) away. This is one of ten members of the heron family that regularly feed in the marsh. Each species has its own way of foraging.

Great egrets stalk slowly and then grab their prey with a sudden jab. Snowy egrets may shuffle their golden feet to attract fish or run in short bursts, spreading their wings and moving about quickly to catch up with small fish. Reddish egrets from the southern marshes are the dancers of the marsh mud flats. They spread their wings, turn, and run about as they feed on fish, looking quite comical.

Herons and egrets use sticks to build messy nests in trees, often on islands surrounded by marsh. Most live in large colonies. Several species of wading birds will nest together, making an unbelievable racket.

Ospreys are the most common raptors breeding in the salt marsh. They nest in or near marshes, where they build big nests made of sticks in dead trees, on utility poles, or on high platforms that people have built for them. Ospreys rarely eat anything but fish. They fly over marsh creeks and nearby open water, sometimes hovering to spot a fish. As they dive headfirst and plunge into the water, the birds reach out with their feet at the last second to grab their prey with their talons. Rough pads on their feet help them hold onto their slippery prey.

An osprey family nests on a platform in the marsh.

Salt Marsh Specialists

More than any other song, the cackling call of the clapper rail reminds us of the salt marsh. If you wake up early, it is easy to hear this noisy pigeon-sized bird. Seeing one is another matter. It spends much of its time hidden in cordgrass. The best way to spot one is to wait quietly, partly hidden, along a salt marsh creek. At low tide the rail may strut out of the grass in search of fiddler crabs, its favorite food. It builds a nest of dead grass in the tall cordgrass and bends live grass over the

A clapper rail catches a worm on a salt marsh mud flat.

nest for a roof. The clapper rail is a salt marsh specialist—that is, it has adapted to live its entire life in the marsh.

Two sparrows are also salt marsh specialists. Seaside sparrows can be heard from every direction in spring and summer, singing their buzzing song from a tall grass stalk or a stick in the marsh. They construct a little cup nest just above the high-tide level among marsh grasses. Seaside sparrows feed in open muddy areas and along edges of marsh creeks. In addition to insects and seeds, which are typical sparrow

The saltmarsh sharp-tailed sparrow (left) is one of two bird species found only in salt marshes.

A male seaside sparrow (right) sings its buzzing song.

25

An American oystercatcher approaches its nest built in dead, washed-up cordgrass called wrack.

food, they eat many small crabs and snails. In winter, seaside sparrows from northern salt marshes fly to marshes in the South, where their main food is seeds—especially the seeds of smooth cordgrass.

The saltmarsh sharp-tailed sparrow is a much quieter bird and harder to see. In the spring, males often perch on the taller cordgrass at the edges of creeks. They nest between grass stalks just above the ground. During the highest tides, their nests are often flooded and destroyed. Birds that lay their eggs just after a new moon, when the highest tides have passed, have the best chance of success. They have just enough time to incubate their eggs and raise their young to leave the nest before the next new moon—and highest high tide—four weeks later.

Birds in Black and White

With a bold black-and-white pattern and a huge, dazzling orange-red beak and eye-ring, the American oystercatcher looks like the clown of the marsh. Oystercatchers fly around in small, noisy flocks during the spring, pointing their beaks down while calling loudly. The long, chisel-shaped beak is useful for jamming between shells of a tasty mussel or oyster.

Another noisy shorebird with a bold black-and-white wing

pattern is the willet. Its call, *pill-will-willet*, is one of the most memorable sounds of the salt marsh. If you walk any distance through the shorter smooth cordgrass in late spring, you are bound to flush a willet off its nest. It lays four olive-colored eggs speckled with dark flecks. The eggs are pointy on one end, and they are neatly arranged in the nest with all eggs pointing toward the center. They fit tightly in the nest, and the willet can incubate them evenly.

When the tide fills marsh creeks, you can look for another black-and-white bird. The black skimmer forages by flying with its orange knifelike mandible (the lower half of the beak) skimming the surface of the water. When the mandible hits a fish, the fish is scooped up by the force of the water. Then the skimmer snaps its beak shut, clamping down on the fish. No other bird feeds in this manner.

A willet uses its bold black-and-white wings for a courtship display.

28   *A laughing gull chick breaks through its egg with help from its egg tooth, the sharp, tiny white projection on its beak. Once the chick has hatched, the egg tooth will fall off.*

Chapter 2

A female salt marsh mosquito fills up on blood from the author's arm.

SUMMER
Reign of the Bloodsuckers

As SPRING COMES TO AN END, LAUGHING GULL chicks are hatching. Summer welcomes many other baby birds into the world. But from our point of view it also brings unwelcome swarms of biting insects. Salt marshes are not always the most pleasant places to be. A few bad apples of the insect world can spoil a day in the marsh.

Salt marsh mosquitoes are present through most of the warm season. In some marshes, they fly about in clouds. The females seek our blood to get enough nutrients to lay hundreds of eggs. Their larvae are among the relatively few insects that can live in salt water. Salt marsh mosquitoes lay their eggs in shallow pools in the upper marsh. The eggs hatch into larvae, which grow for only a few days before metamorphosing into pupae. After a day or so, the pupae metamorphose once again to become adults.

Greenhead flies use their excellent vision to find us visitors to the marsh.

In many places, local governments have tried to get rid of mosquitoes by digging ditches in the marsh to drain the pools where mosquitoes breed. This approach has rarely worked, but it has scarred huge amounts of marsh and harmed habitat for ducks and other marsh creatures.

Ouch!

In some ways, biting midges are even worse than mosquitoes. They look like little black dots, each one the size of the period at the end of this sentence. Their bites can itch for days. Biting midges are hard to swat, and they crawl up your sleeves and into your hair.

You might vote for greenheads to be named the biggest pain in the marsh. Greenheads are a kind of horsefly. When they spy someone with their huge, green compound eyes, they fly in for a meal. Quickly, a big cloud of greenheads gather, each fly trying to land and slice its sawlike mouthparts into your skin. A few painful bites might be enough to drive you out of the marsh. Diving into the bay won't help. The swarm will be waiting when you surface.

Within the female greenhead's first few days as an adult, she produces her first batch of one hundred to two hundred eggs. She lays these on plants over the marsh mud, where the larvae will live. In order to lay more eggs, she needs protein from your blood. After hatching from the eggs, the larvae prey on other little creatures in the mud. They spend the winter deep in the mud and go into the resting stage as pupae late in spring. In early summer they metamorphose to flying adults, driving visitors from the marsh.

More Marsh Plants

A breezy day, when the biting insects are not flying as much as on a calm day, is a good time to take a look at the plants growing in the high marsh. This part of the marsh floods only during the highest tides.

Salt-meadow cordgrass grows mostly in the high marsh. This bright, spring-green grass is very fine. By summer, this grass looks like a foot-high lawn that has flattened to the ground. Salt-meadow cordgrass shares this high-marsh habitat with another low-growing grass, salt grass. You can tell salt grass from salt-meadow cordgrass because it has many more leaves, which go up the grass stem on alternate sides. These short grasses were once used as hay to feed livestock. Many a horse got stuck in the marsh while mowing this "salt hay."

This soft flattened grass is salt-meadow cordgrass found in the upper marsh.

31

A male red-winged blackbird calls atop a marsh elder plant in the high marsh.

Higher in the marsh, in places the tide rarely reaches, a few kinds of shrubs grow. Two of the most common are marsh elder and groundsel tree. Groundsel tree is actually a bush. In autumn it is covered with white cottonlike seeds. Marsh elder fruits are small and green. The few bushes that grow in the high marsh are important to some marsh birds. Red-winged blackbirds and marsh wrens often nest in these bushes. Many birds use these bushes as singing posts. They are the highest places a bird can perch to announce its territory.

Rampaging Reed

In many places you will see dense stands of grass that you can barely walk through. The common reed, which is also known by its scientific name, *Phragmites* (frag-MY-tees), has stalks about one inch (two and a half centimeters) thick. It is often about 10 feet (3 meters) high, though it can grow as tall as 20 feet (6 meters). *Phragmites* has taken over large areas of salt marsh, eliminating and replacing cordgrasses and other marsh plants. *Phragmites* often gets a foothold in places where the marsh has been disturbed. For example, if mud and sand are dredged from a boat channel and dumped on the marsh, *Phragmites* will grow on the dirt pile. From there it will start to take over part of the marsh. Like cordgrass, it spreads by growing underground stems called rhizomes. These can be up to 20 feet (6 meters) long. New shoots of grass grow up from rhizomes, and the colony of *Phragmites* expands in all directions.

Few plants can grow among dense reeds. Few animals live in the middle of big stands. However, marsh wrens favor the edge of reed beds for nesting. You can hear their long, gurgling rattle. The firm stalks of *Phragmites* are perfect for the wren's ball-shaped nest with a side entrance. Marsh wrens build several nests in a season, but nest in only one at a time. The rest may be made to fool predators into searching for wren eggs in the wrong places. Red-winged blackbirds eat seeds that grow from the reeds' plumelike flower stalks. In late summer, huge flocks of purple martins and barn swallows roost in reed beds at night. The dense growth makes it harder for predators to find and attack them.

Phragmites does best where water is not too salty and where the tide covers the roots only briefly. In deeper water, smooth cordgrass still reigns. But almost all other marsh plants have suffered big losses of habitat to this invasive weed, which came

A marsh wren emerges from its nest in the common reeds.

Purple martins flock by the thousands in late summer and roost in dense stands of common reed.

A flock of sandpipers called greater yellowlegs rest on a New Jersey mud flat during their southbound migration.

from either Europe, Asia, or Africa. There is actually a native variety of *Phragmites*, which is similar but not as invasive, but it is hard to find because most of its habitat has been taken over by its alien relative.

Time to Wander

By midsummer, laughing gulls are on the move again. Once the young ones are raised, some gulls leave the nesting areas to wander many miles north or south along the shore. Many seek out landfills, where they fill up on garbage. The abundance of garbage dumps is one reason why laughing

A three-month-old laughing gull flies over the marsh.

gulls are now so common. In the late 1800s and early 1900s, many colonies were destroyed by eggers—people hunting for eggs to sell for food. Many gulls were also shot for their feathers, which were popular in ladies' fashions at that time. Laws to protect them and lots of garbage have helped bring gulls back.

By midsummer, sandpipers that have flown to the Arctic are starting to return to feed on the mud flats before continuing south. Adults are the first to arrive, but before summer is over this year's crop of juveniles will start to arrive. When the tide is low, they seem to feed madly, but they rest in tight groups on islands or beaches when the tide is high.

Glasswort lights up the salt marsh in autumn.

Chapter 3

By late summer, a laughing gull has lost its black head feathers.

AUTUMN
From Green to Gold

AS AUTUMN BEGINS, A LAUGHING GULL is no longer so handsome. The adult's black head feathers have all but disappeared. The red beak and legs have turned blackish. In early autumn, young laughing gulls are mostly brownish. They are learning to survive, but it is a dangerous time. The young gulls must quickly learn to find food and avoid enemies.

Autumn brings relief from greenheads, so we can venture into the marsh again. Early fall is a good time to study the rest of the insects of the marsh. Compared with a freshwater marsh, a salt marsh doesn't have as many species of insects, but the total number of insects can be surprising. Sweep a butterfly net back and forth through the marsh grasses and you will pick up many small green mirid bugs, katydids, and planthoppers. The mirid bugs and planthoppers use their

A salt marsh meadow katydid clings to cordgrass.

A mirid bug sucks sap from cordgrass while a spider is camouflaged above.

strawlike mouths to suck juices from grass stems. Katydids chew on the grass leaves. Some insects are not so easy to catch, such as the seaside dragonlet, a small dragonfly that does us a favor by eating salt marsh mosquitoes and other flying insects.

In the high marsh, several plants flower at this time of year, attracting insects with their nectar. Mixed in with the salt grass is sea lavender. Its tiny purple flowers attract two butterflies that are salt marsh specialists. The salt marsh skipper is a tiny, plain-looking butterfly whose caterpillars feed on salt grass. The broad-winged skipper is a little larger. Its caterpillars eat *Phragmites*. Both of these butterflies pollinate sea lavender when moving from flower to flower to feed on nectar.

The brightest color in the marsh comes not from flowers but from glasswort. This fleshy, edible plant turns orange, purple, or red in fall. It grows best in bare spots on the marsh, where there is less competition from other plants. It is crunchy and salty and is sometimes used in salads.

Migration

As marsh grasses turn from green to golden, it is time for many marsh birds to move on. Laughing gulls in the northern states join in flocks during midautumn. They will head south where they can find more food in winter. Many laughing gulls migrate to marshes and beaches along the coast of the Gulf of Mexico. Others spend much of their time over the open waters of the Gulf itself. Young laughing gulls tend to go the farthest. Many travel as far as South America for the winter.

Let's fly with the laughing gulls for a look at some salt marshes along the way. As the flock of gulls wings south down the Atlantic Coast, it is never far from salt marshes. Along most of the coast, the ocean beaches are on barrier islands. These are usually long skinny islands of sand. The ocean is on one side and a shallow bay or lagoon on the other. On the quieter bay side, the island is usually fringed by salt marsh.

When we arrive in North Carolina, the barrier islands bow way out into the ocean. From here south, in the fresher parts of the estuaries, alligators are visible. We also start to see new birds in the marsh. White ibises with their long, curved, bright-red bills and haunting blue eyes are common in southern marshes.

A broad-winged skipper (left) sips nectar from sea lavender. Caterpillars of this butterfly feed only on common reed.

The caterpillar of the salt marsh skipper (right) eats only salt grass.

Farther down the coast in South Carolina and Georgia, the salt marshes are wider—and at their liveliest. Salt marshes here grow year-round, producing a great deal of life. In fact, if you weighed a year's growth of all the plants on one acre of marsh here, it would weigh more than a year's growth on an acre of almost any other ecosystem or environment.

White ibis are commonly seen in southern marshes.

Gulls Go Gulfward

Soon, many of the gulls veer west and head for the Gulf Coast, while the rest winter in the Caribbean or eastern Florida. We follow the westbound gulls past the Florida panhandle, Alabama, and Mississippi and fly into Louisiana.

Louisiana has some of the largest marshes in the country. But much is being lost. Channels dug into the marsh to haul oil-drilling equipment have opened the marsh to erosion. Levees on the Mississippi River have also done much damage. Levees are man-made walls, usually made of dirt, built along the sides of rivers to control floods. They also prevent the mud carried by the river from flooding onto the marsh. The marsh needs the mud because this whole area is slowly sinking and sea level is slowly rising. The mud builds up the marsh to a level where grasses can continue to survive.

Marshes in Louisiana and elsewhere help protect us from the worst effects of hurricanes. Marshes slow the flooding caused by strong winds, because each grass stalk holds back a tiny bit of water flowing into shore. Multiply that by millions of grass stalks and that is enough to make a big difference.

Where the marsh is wide, flood damage is reduced. Hurricanes lose much of their energy as soon as they hit land. Wide stretches of marsh once separated the city of New Orleans from the sea. Much of that marsh has been destroyed, and what was once marsh is now open water. Damage to cities on the Gulf Coast by Hurricane Katrina in 2005 might not have been as bad as it was if the marshes had still been there. Now there is much interest in restoring those marshes.

The gulls fly west along the Gulf of Mexico and on to Texas, where this flock will spend the winter. Many of the Gulf marshes are sandier and easier to walk through than northern salt marshes. They have even more wading birds than northern salt marshes have. Bubble-gum-pink roseate spoonbills swish their bizarre, spoon-shaped bills back and forth in the shallow water. When they feel their prey—small fish and invertebrates—they snap their beaks shut. Ragged-crested reddish egrets practically dance on the mud flats as they run, turn, and spread their wings this way and that, stabbing at fish in the shallows.

A roseate spoonbill takes off in a Texas salt marsh.

A black skimmer fishes, slicing through the surface of the water with its knifelike bill.

Chapter 4

This sailfin mollie lives in a Texas salt marsh pool.

WINTER
Warm Gulf Waters

WATER TEMPERATURES ALONG THE GULF COAST never reach freezing, so there is much more activity there in winter than in the North. Fish are still very active.

Many of the fish in the marsh are different from those in the New Jersey marshes. One of these—the sailfin mollie, a familiar aquarium fish—can be found in shallow salt marsh waters.

Swarms of water boatmen swim in shallow pools. These insects belong to the group called true bugs. Along with the salt marsh mosquitoes, they are among the few insects adapted to life in salt water.

Many fish and shrimp use the southern salt marsh as a nursery. Marsh grasses, oyster beds, and marsh channels make good places to hide from larger fish. Plenty of invertebrates,

such as grass shrimp, amphipods, and worms, live in the marsh, feeding young fish. Shrimp eat bits of decomposing plants and animals, called detritus, along with many detritus-eating animals.

The marsh is also an important nursery ground for young blue crabs. Though they are born in deeper waters, the tiny crabs float with the tides into the marsh to spend much of their time there. Aside from providing us with tasty chowder, the crabs are useful in protecting the marsh by eating lots of periwinkle snails. Scientists have shown that when blue crabs are fenced out of a patch of cordgrass, the periwinkles may eat all of the grass. When people harvest too many crabs, periwinkles can eat and destroy the marsh.

A periwinkle is a roundish snail, often found on the cordgrass. With its sawlike mouthpart called a radula, the snail slices into grass leaves. It eats parts of the living leaf, but the slices allow fungi to get in, killing and decaying the rest of the leaf. The periwinkles may later dine on the decaying grass with the fungi.

Blue crabs (left) are important prey of many fish, turtles, otters, and people. They are also predators of snails, fish, and oysters.

When abundant, periwinkles (right) can destroy large areas of salt marsh.

Sun Signals Return

As winter draws to an end, the days grow warmer and longer on the Gulf. Marsh birds start to sing. Herons, egrets, and spoonbills gather near their nesting islands. They will feed their young with the abundant life of the marsh.

We saw how the sun drives the flow of energy in the marsh that feeds this life. It also drives many life cycles. As winter continues, the sun stays up longer each day. Longer days trigger a change inside the gulls' bodies—a signal that it is time to migrate. Flocks of gulls will make their way back along the coast and return north. Now, those of us in the North will keep an eye and an ear out for the return of the laughing gulls and the spring renewal of life in the marsh.

The return of the laughing gull makes the salt marsh a livelier place.

What Causes the Tides?

Tides are caused by gravity—mainly by the pull of the moon. We are used to the idea that Earth's gravity pulls on the moon, keeping the moon in orbit around Earth. But the moon's gravity also pulls on Earth.

How does the moon's pull cause ocean tides on Earth from so far away? The answer begins with the fact that gravity pulls harder on close objects than it does on things that are farther away. Earth is so wide that the moon's pull is much stronger on the near side of the planet than it is on the far side.

Since water flows freely on Earth's surface, the difference in gravitational pull is easy to see in the oceans. All of the oceans are connected to one another, and they form a layer of water on Earth's surface, broken here and there by continents and islands. Under the pull of the moon, this layer bulges. When the moon is directly above, it pulls on any water that happens to lie below, raising the ocean higher onto the shores. That creates a high tide. At the same time, the solid sphere of Earth moves toward the moon as one huge unit. But the fluid ocean waters on the far side of the planet resist the moon's weaker pull, and more water flows to that side as Earth is tugged through the watery layer. That creates another high tide on the far side of Earth. These slight bulges in the oceans draw water away from other places around Earth, lowering the oceans in those places and creating low tides.

As Earth turns and the moon passes over different parts of the planet, the ocean levels rise and fall, causing two high tides and two low tides with each rotation. This effect on daily life from an object so far away is one of nature's marvels.

On some days, the tides go higher and lower than at other times because the pull of the sun also creates ocean tides. (The sun's effect is smaller because it is much farther away.) Tides are greatest during the new moon, when the moon is dark and the sun and moon are on the same side of Earth. The tides are almost as great during the full moon, when the sun and moon are on opposite sides of Earth. The tides don't rise as high or drop as low during the other phases of the moon, when the moon, the sun, and Earth are not lined up.

Glossary

amphipod—a small, bottom-living shrimplike crustacean that is somewhat flattened from side to side.

brackish—refers to water that is somewhat salty, but not as salty as seawater.

crustacean—an animal with a tough exoskeleton, or outer covering, jointed legs, and antennae, such as a crab, a shrimp, or an amphipod.

detritus—bits of dead decomposing plants and animals.

estuary—a place, such as a bay or river mouth, where fresh water flows into and mixes with salt water.

food chain—the sequence of what eats what in a particular environment.

lagoon—a shallow body of salty or brackish water separated from the sea by a narrow strip of land.

levee—a high man-made bank built along a river to keep the water from flooding nearby areas.

metamorphose—to change from one life stage to another, such as from a pupa to an adult fly.

migration—the seasonal movement of animals from one area to another.

mummichog—a small marsh-dwelling fish that is a member of the killifish group.

Phragmites—the scientific name for the group of tall wetland grasses that includes the common reed.

protein—a nutrient needed by all cells that helps build all parts of the body.

rhizome—an underground stem of grasses and some other plants from which shoots grow.

Spartina—the scientific name of a group of marsh grasses.

wetland—an area where plants grow that is covered by water for at least part of the year.

Suggested Reading

Kurtz, Kevin. *A Day in the Salt Marsh*. Mount Pleasant, SC: Sylvan Dell, 2007.

Lippson, Alice Jane, and Robert L. Lippson. *Life in the Chesapeake Bay*. 3rd ed. Baltimore: Johns Hopkins University Press, 2006.

Wechsler, Doug. *Ospreys*. The Really Wild Life of Birds of Prey series. New York: PowerKids Press, 2001.

Web Site for Students*

Salt Marsh Life. www.saltmarshlife.com

Web Sites for Teachers*

BTNEP Estuary Resources (Barataria Terrebonne National Estuary Program's On Line Estuary Education Resource Module). educators.btnep. org/Resources/resource.asp?id=66

Dreyer, Glenn D., and William A. Niering, eds. *Tidal Marshes of Long Island Sound: Ecology, History, and Restoration*. The Connecticut College Arboretum. arboretum.conncoll.edu/publications/34/FRAME.HTM

* Active at the time of publication

Index

*Page numbers in **bold** refer to captions.*